What Is It Worth?

by Susan Buntrock

Illustrated by Christy Hale

HAMPTON-BROWN

Tisha and her neighbors are having a yard sale.

Tisha wants to sell some old toys. One of the toys is a doll.

The doll is made of wood. It is dirty and old. Its arms and legs do not move. Its eyes do not open and close.

"What a boring doll!" says Tisha. "It does not do anything. It is not pretty."

People come to the yard sale. They look at Tisha's toys.

"This is an interesting doll," says one man. "I will buy it for my daughter. I will give you ten dollars for it."

Tisha thinks ten dollars is a lot of money for an old doll.

Next, a woman comes to look at the toys.

"The beads on this doll are beautiful. I will give you twenty dollars for the doll," she says.

Tisha is excited. "Twenty dollars!" she thinks. "That is a lot of money for an old doll."

Another woman comes to the table. She looks
at the doll for a long time.

"Where did you get this doll?" she asks.

"I found it in a box. It was in our basement," says Tisha. "This lady wants to buy it for twenty dollars!"

"This doll is worth more than that," explains
the woman.
"What do you mean?" asks Tisha.

"I work in a museum," says the woman. "We have dolls like this one. The doll was made a long time ago. It is probably from East Africa."

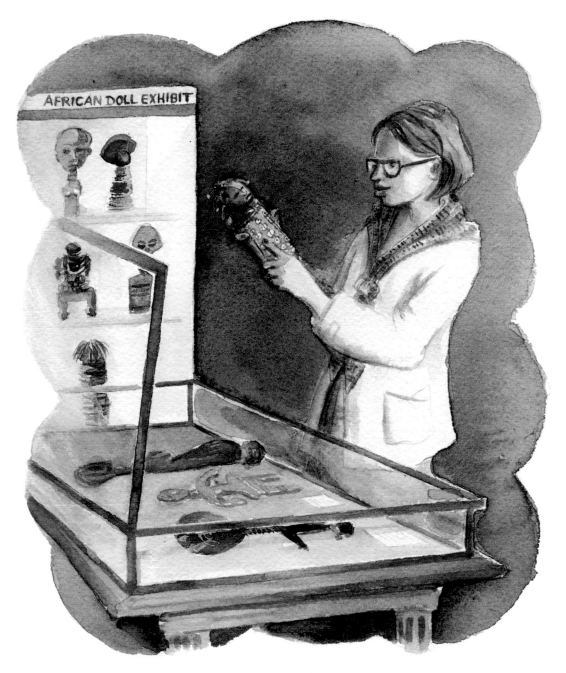

"In Africa, dolls are more than just toys," the
woman continues.

"Someone made this doll for a special person,"
she says. "There is no other doll like it in the world."

"Wow!" Tisha thinks. "I am sorry," she says to the people at the yard sale. "This special doll is not for sale! Some things are worth more than money."